CRICUT EXPLORE AIR 2

The Ultimate Beginners Guide to Master Your Cricut Explore Air 2, Design Space and Tips and Tricks to Realize Your Project Ideas

Emily Maker

© **Copyright 2020 - All rights reserved.**

The content contained within this book may not be reproduced, duplicated or transmitted without direct written permission from the author or the publisher.

Under no circumstances will any blame or legal responsibility be held against the publisher, or author, for any damages, reparation, or monetary loss due to the information contained within this book. Either directly or indirectly.

Legal Notice: This book is copyright protected. This book is only for personal use. You cannot amend, distribute, sell, use, quote or paraphrase any part, or the content within this book, without the consent of the author or publisher.

Disclaimer Notice: Please note the information contained within this document is for educational and entertainment purposes only. All effort has been executed to present accurate, up to date, and reliable, complete information. No warranties of any kind are declared or implied. Readers acknowledge that the author is not engaging in the rendering of legal, financial, medical or professional advice. The content within this book has been derived from various sources. Please consult a licensed professional before attempting any techniques outlined in this book. By reading this document, the reader agrees that under no circumstances is the author responsible for any losses, direct or indirect, which are incurred as a result of the use of information contained within this document, including, but not limited to, — errors, omissions, or inaccuracies.

TABLE OF CONTENTS

INTRODUCTION 4

CHAPTER 1 WHAT IS CRICUT? 9

CHAPTER 2 HOW TO SET UP YOUR CRICUT MACHINE 17

CHAPTER 3 THE BEST MATERIALS FOR CRICUT 26

CHAPTER 4 PROJECTS ON THE CRICUT EXPLORE AIR 2 35

CHAPTER 5 MAKING MONEY WITH CRICUT 46

CHAPTER 6 HELPFUL TROUBLESHOOTING TECHNIQUES 56

CHAPTER 7 HACKS, TIPS, AND TECHNIQUES 65

CHAPTER 8 TIPS AND TRICKS, YOU NEED TO KNOW TO MAKE CRICUT MACHINE MUCH EASIER AND EFFICIENT 71

CHAPTER 9 THINGS TO KNOW ABOUT CRICUT 79

CHAPTER 10 TOOLS AND ACCESSORIES OF CRICUT MACHINE 89

CHAPTER 11 FAQ 98

CONCLUSION 106

Introduction

The Cricut Explore Air 2 can be regarded as an electronic cutter or a personal crafting machine that can be used in the cutting of different materials such as cardstock, vinyl, Faux leather, Magnet sheets, sticker paper, Vellum, Fabric, Sticker Paper, etc.

The Cricut Explore Air 2 can make use of the pen and markers in writing, drawing as well as scoring your project with a nifty score tool. The machine can also be used in printing and cutting.

The Cricut Explore Air 2 is an electronic cutting machine that makes use of a precise blade as well as a series of rollers in cutting out images, just anything you can imagine. It is used in cutting out fancy paper shapes as well as fonts that came on cartridges.

The Cricut Explore Air has evolved, and now instead of making use of the cartridges, they have a library of cut files. You can also get your files uploaded and then cut them. The good thing about the machine now is that you can design your project with the use of the Cricut Design Space software, after which the material to be used is placed on the cutting mat before confirming the settings, and you are then good to go.

It is now able to provide a platform where it can be used for drawing, scoring, and engraving; it can be used on over a hundred materials. It is designed to cut whatever material you are working with correctly.

This machine can be used for scrapbooking a sphere, DIY, decoration designs, party ideas, crafts, etc.

Unboxing the Cricut Explore Air 2 Machine

After purchasing the Cricut Explore Air 2 machine, it is essential to make sure it has all its accessories completely boxed in and nothing is missing. If you find anything missing, you are advised to return it to where it was purchased or simply contact Cricut support and inform them about the missing accessories.

A complete packaged Cricut Explore Air 2 machine should have the following items in it:

- Cricut Explore Air 2
- Instruction manual
- Cricut cutting mat
- Cutting blade
- Silver pen and the accessory adapter
- Power and the USB cords
- The Cardstock and the Vinyl samples

It is to be noted that we have different kinds available, and depending on the kits you purchased, your Cricut Explore Air 2 machine might come with extra items included in it. The following are different kinds of packages available for the Cricut Explore Air 2 machine:

- Ultimate Kit

- Tools Kit

- Vinyl starter Kit

- Complete Starter Kit

- The Premium Vinyl

Different Parts of the Cricut Explore Air 2

Cutting Mat

The Cutting Mat gives a platform on how the materials are going to be laid into the Cricut Machine. It helps in getting the material securely placed by being sticky, holds on firmly to the material.

Tool Cup

The tool cup is the part that holds scissors, pens, and other Cricut tools in use. The pen is used by opening the accessory clamp A and placing the pen in it, after which the clamp is closed.

Accessory Storage Compartments

Apart from the Tool Cup, the Cricut Explore Air 2 machine is made up of two compartments that are also used in holding tools, these are:

- Smaller Compartment

- Larger Compartment

The smaller compartment is positioned at the left for holding additional blade housings, the accessory adapter as well as the blades. The smaller chamber is made up of a magnetic strip for securely keeping the replacement blades and prevent them from rolling.

The larger compartment is used to store longer tools and pens.

Accessory Clamp A

The accessory clamp A comes pre-installed as the accessory adapter, and the pen for drawing instead of having to cut can be inserted through this part. It also helps in holding the scoring blades.

Blade Clamp A

Cricut Explore Air Machine has the Blade clamp A already pre-installed in them. The replacement or the removal of bits of vinyl can also be done here.

Smart Set Dial

The Cricut Explore Air machine, through its fast mode of operation, enables the user to turn and indicate which material is to be cut with the twice fast mode with the use of the Smart Set dial. All you need to do is rotate the Smart Set dial and choose the material you will be cutting.

Removing and Replacing the Accessory and the Blade Clamps of the Cricut Explore Air Machine

To remove the accessory clamp or blade, pull open the lever, after which you will then get the metal housing pulled out.

The blade is positioned seated inside; having a tiny plunger on the top, pressing this down will reveal the blade which is held out magnetically.

To get the blade replaced, if the need arises, all you have to do is to get the blade pulled out and drop the new blade in.

Chapter 1 What Is Cricut?

Cricut is a popular brand of machine roaming each time in the country. It's a unique and exciting gadget used by many people who wish to make amazing and creative projects. As of these days, you will find 3 distinct versions of Cricut: The Cricut Create Machine, top Cricut Expression, not to mention the starting version Cricut Personal Electronic Cutter Machine.

The Cricut machine has been developed for a wide range of factors. Today most people may believe that this device is exclusively for creating scrapbooks, but it's not. The Cricut machine may be utilized for much more than creating scrapbooks. In case your creativity shuts down on a Cricut machine, you are able to use a lot of great Cricut tips that will help you and make everything easier for you.

Before accentuating concerning what Cricut can help the culture, let's check out the brief history of Cricut itself. Cricut was initially manufactured by a big business called Provo Craft, which was previously a tiny shop. Approximately forty years back, airers4you of Provo Craft began as a local store in the tiny town of Provo, Utah. With their creativity and resourcefulness, airers4you finally expanded after several years. Today, they now have a total of 10 retailers with almost as much as 200,000 feet distribution facility.

Should you glance at the standard Cricut machine, it is like the look of an inkjet printer?

However, it does not require a laptop to be operated at all. Also, an average individual can use the function since it does not need programming talents as well. Among its advantages is the fact that it is lightweight.

The blade may even cut thin and thick papers ranging between one inch as well as 5.5 inches in height.

Cricut just weighs 12 "pounds, including the power adapter. Moreover, you are able to carry it anywhere, for example, party gatherings or maybe case presentations, since it's a transportable product. With their smooth and unique design, it'll regularly seem suitable to the crafting workplace.

It can cut from one to 5.5 inches, but that is not the sole feature it contains. It is capable of lowering headings and edges almost as much as 11 inches in length, which makes it a great match to a newspaper with a dimension of 12x12 inches. Unlike any other brand, the main facet of Cricut is to maintain the ability to cut a lot of materials. Cricut can also cut a newspaper that has a wide range of up to 0.5 mm in density. Fortunately, Provo Craft has supplied additional components such as designer paper pads as well as card stock pads that can be used in conjunction with the Cricut cartridges. In reality, these 2 various forms of papers are made to get a great match with Cricut.

Present Models

These versions are now compatible with the present Cricut design space program.

Cricut Research 1

The explore it's really a wired die-cutting tool that can cut an assortment of materials from paper to cloth and much more. Be aware: there's a wireless Bluetooth adapter available for sale individually. This machine just had one instrument slot machine compared with other currently supported versions that have 2.

Cricut Research Air

The explore air is really a wireless die-cutting machine that may cut many different materials from paper to cloth and much more. This system is basically the same as its next iteration, aside from the home and slower cutting skills.

Cricut Maker

The maker is your sole Cricut machine which supports the usage of a blade for cutting edge cloth directly and also a steering wheel with varying pressure to score heavier papers compared to the initial scoring stylus.

Cricut Expression

The Cricut expression® provides several benefits over the former version. To begin with, it permits users to reduce shapes and fonts in a variety between 1/4" into 231/2" and has a 12" x 12" cutting edge with flexible slides so users no longer will need to trim down their media to 6" x 12". It cuts a larger assortment of substances, such as vellum, cloth, chipboard, vinyl, and thin foils. Additionally, it offers an LCD display to preview the job and contains features such as amount and auto-fill. Even a "paper saver" style and selection of portrait or landscape orientation also have been included. The fundamental version has two capsules within the buy, plantin schoolbook along with accent essentials.

Cricut Picture

This system was unique because it had an hp 97 inkjet printer built to it that it may either cut and publish pictures. This system had a revamped touch screen interface, also has been extremely big and heavy. The device had a very short lifetime of nearly 1 year.

Cricut Expression Two

The Cricut Expression 2 includes an upgraded exterior from that the Cricut expression. It includes a 12" x 12" cutting mat. This system doesn't have the keyboard the first Cricut along with also the Cricut expression consumed. Instead, it sports a brand new full-color LCD touch display. The LCD touch screen shows the computer keyboard on the display and lets you view where your pictures are going to be on the mat before cutting. Additionally, it has the newest characteristic of independent picture sizing and picture turning directly over the LCD display.

Cricut Mini

The Cricut Mini is a tiny private electronic cutting machine. Unlike other Cricut machines, it simply works using a pc, it cannot cut pictures standing independently. You need to utilize Cricut craft room layout computer software. The Cricut mini includes over 500 pictures automatically unlocked once you join your Cricut using all the Cricut craft room design applications or your Cricut gypsy apparatus. The machine will not have a cartridge jack compatible with Cricut cartridges, except for the Cricut picture capsules. The Cricut mini also offers an exceptional mat dimension of 8.5" x 12". The Cricut mini may cut pictures in a selection of 1/4" into 11 1/2". Even the Cricut mini relied solely on utilizing the Cricut craft room, computer software that no longer works. Of the legacy Cricut machines, the mini is the only one that is outdated and not usable at all. As no recourse has been supplied to the clients who had bought cartridges for that system, Provo-craft has become the focus of several complaints from clients who had been left without recourse with this sudden pressured 'sun-setting' of this machine.

Cartridges

Designs are produced from components saved on capsules. Each cartridge includes a computer keyboard overlay and an education booklet. The plastic computer keyboard overlay suggests key collections for this chance only. Nevertheless, lately, Provo craft has published a "universal overlay" that can be used with cartridges released after August 1, 2013. The objective of the universal overlay would be to simplify the practice of clipping by simply needing to learn 1 keyboard overlay rather than being required to find out the overlay for every individual cartridge. Designs could be cut on a pc using all the Cricut design studio applications, on a USB attached gypsy device, or could be directly inputted onto the Cricut device employing the computer keyboard overlay. There are two forms of cartridges font and shape. Each cartridge has many different creative attributes that could allow for countless distinct cuts from only 1 cartridge. There are over 275 capsules that can be found (separately from the system), including shapes and fonts, together with new ones added each month. A cartridge bought for a stop machine is very likely to turn useless by the point that the machine is stopped. Cricut reserves the right to stop support several versions of the applications at any moment, which may make some capsules instantly obsolete.

What Can Be a Cricut Machine?

The Cricut Explore Air is a die-cutting system (aka craft plotter or cutting-edge system). You can consider it as a printer; you also make an image or layout on your personal computer and then ship it to your device. Except instead of printing your design, the Cricut machine cuts out of whatever substance you desire! The Cricut research air can reduce paper, vinyl, cloth, craft foam, decal paper, faux leather, and longer!

In reality, if you would like to utilize a Cricut just like a printer, then it may do this also! There's an attachment slot on your system and you're able to load a mark in there after which possess the Cricut "draw" the layout for you. It is ideal for obtaining a stunning handwritten look if your design is not all that good.

The Cricut explore air may reduce stuff around 12" broad and includes a little cutting blade mounted within the system. When you are prepared to cut out something, you load the stuff on a sticky mat and then load the mat to your machine. The mat holds the material in place while the Cricut blade moves over the substance and cuts. If it finishes, then you unload the mat in the machine, then peel your project off the mat, and then you are all set to move!

Using a Cricut system, the options are infinite! All you want is a Cricut system, design space, something to reduce, along with your creativity!

What Could I Do with a Cricut Machine?

There are a lot of things you can perform using a Cricut device! There is no way that I could list all of the possibilities, however, here are a couple of popular kinds of jobs to provide you a good concept about exactly what the machine could perform.

· Cut out interesting shapes and letters to get cartoon

· Make a habit, handmade cards for any specific

· Layout a onesie or some t-shirt

- Create a leather necklace

- Create buntings and other party decorations

- Make your stencils for painting

- Create a plastic decal for your vehicle window

- Tag material on your cabinet or in a playroom

- Make monogram cushions

- Make your Christmas decorations

- Address an envelope

- Decorate a mug cup or tumbler

- Etch glass at the house

- Make your wall stickers

- Create a painted wooden signal

- Create your own window

- Cut appliqués or quilt squares

- Produce stickers to get a rack mixer

...and plenty of different jobs that are too many to list!

Chapter 2 How to Set Up Your Cricut Machine

Using a Cricut machine is a very simple task and does not require a lot of effort. It is relatively short and compact like a printer, so it does not need a lot of space to sit. However, the machine needs to have some space, approximately 10 inches, both front and back, to allow free movement of the rollers. It is not heavy and can be easily placed on a desk or a crafting table. The computer which you will use should have the Design Space software installed. After purchasing a brand new Cricut maker, take note of the contents of the box. The device comes with power cords, one mat, and a blade. Following are the instructions to set up the machine:

How to Plug in the Device?

First, the Cricut machine needs to be plugged into the computer and also the power outlet. Use the USB cable provided to connect the computer to the machine. Next to the USB cable, the power port should be connected to both the outlet and the device, also provided in the packaging. Now press the ON button on the machine. It will illuminate to indicate that it is working.

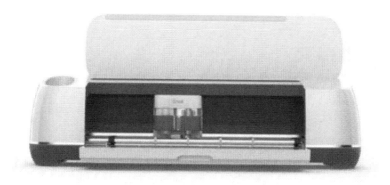

How to Load/Unload the Mat?

For placing your material to cut it on the mat, it's important to know the placement. First, the mat's cover should be removed and placed elsewhere. The Cricut maker comes with a blue LightGrip mat, which is used for cutting paper mainly. The match will be slightly sticky for good placement of the material. When loading, the material should be placed in the top left corner of the mat. Be sure to press down gently so that the material could be evened out. Place the top of the mat in the guides of the machine.

Gently press on the rollers and press the load/to unload the button on top of the Cricut. Once loaded up, the software will tell you the next step. After the project has been finished, the material needs to be unloaded. Press on the load/unload button and take out the mat from the machine. The right way to remove the material from the mat is that it should be placed on a straight surface, and the mat should be peeled off. The remaining scraps can be peeled off by a scrapper or a tweezer.

How to Load/Unload Cricut Pen?

For loading a pen, the machine needs to be opened to show the two clamps. For placement of the pen, clamp A needs to be opened up. Remove the cap on the pen and place it so that the arrow on the pen is facing the front. Gently pull the clamp upwards when placing the pen. Place the pen inside the clamp until the arrow disappears and a click sound is heard. To unload a pen, simply open up clamp A and remove the pen by upward motion. If you do not remove the pen, the machine will not close and the pen cap cannot be put on.

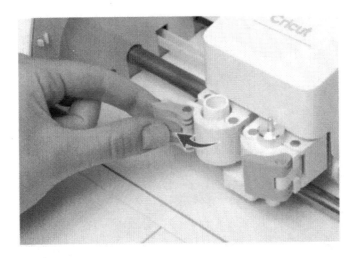

Recently, new specialized pens are available called the Infusible Ink Pen and markers. They work in by sublimation process, completely fusing the ink onto the material. It is best for Iron-on. The difference between it and regular pens is that they leave a thicker line. They also come in in two variations: traditional and neon. Heating is required to use this instrument, which can be achieved by Cricut Easy Press. For using it, first select a blank slot and fit the pen, any blank slot can fit the pens. Then draw your design on design space or by hand. Make sure the image size is according to the Cricut Easy Press. Then place a laser paper in the Cricut Maker or Cricut Explorer. Now use the Infusible Ink to draw in the design. Transfer the image to Cricut Easy Press and follow its guidelines.

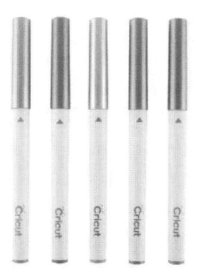

How to Load/Unload Blades?

A Fine point blade comes already place inside the machine when the package is opened. If the project requires a changing of the blade, then first, you need to unload the blade. Open up accessory clamp B and pull it upwards gently. Then pull the blade out of the machine. When putting another blade, i.e., rotary blade, make sure that the gears fit evenly. Once placed, it will give a click sound. Whenever someone is doing a project, the Cricut Maker automatically checks if the right blade is placed. With QuickSwap housing available, it is easier to change blades. Simply press on the housing tip to loosen its grip, and then slide or remove the blades.

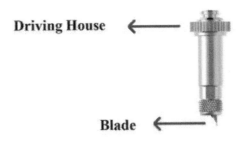

Driving House

Blade

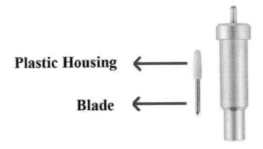

Plastic Housing

Blade

How to Load/Unload a Scoring Stylus?

To load and unload a scoring stylus is just like loading and uploading the pen. Open up the accessory clamp A and put the pen tip downwards while holding up the clamp gently. Place it in until the arrow disappears, and a click sound is made. Now close the clamp and follow the instructions in the software. Once the scoring is completed, the scoring pen needs to be unloaded. Open up the clamp and remove the pen by pulling it upwards.

How to Load or Unload Cartridges?

Cricut Explorer comes with the feature of using cartridges. To use a cartridge first, you need to open up Design Space using our Cricut account. Open up the green account button and click on the link cartridge option. A new page will open, which is the link cartridge window. Now turn on the Cricut Explorer and put the cartridge in the cartridge slot. The cartridge label should be facing forward, and it should be fully set. When the software air recognizes the cartridge in the device, then click 'link cartridge' at the lower right corner of the screen. The screen will confirm whether the cartridge has been linked or not. Now the cartridge can be safely removed. To access the cartridges files, first, you should open Design Space with your Cricut ID. Then click on the ownership icon and select purchased. Now find the cartridge that you are looking for. To insert the items in your cartridge onto a design, on the Design Space window, click on insert and search for the cartridge by name or click on the cartridge icon.

How to Load or Unload a Debossing Tool?

Debossing tool also called a debossing tip, is used to press on the materials, giving it an everlasting imprint. Instead of a solid end, it has a rollerball that allows the color to slide onto the material rather than dragging on. This feature gives sharp images and opens up new possibilities. It is used in the Cricut Maker. It goes into the Quickswap housing and, like any other blade, into clamp B.

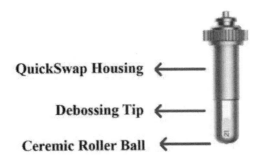

How to Cut Vinyl from A Cricut Machine?

First, place the Vinyl liner side down onto the Standard grip mat. Then put it inside the machine after selecting the design. Push the go button to start.

For a smooth placement of the vinyl, you should use vinyl transfer tape. Transfer tape is a kind of pre-mask that transfers vinyl graphics to a substrate after being cut and weeded.

After cutting is done, remove the negatives of the image by a weeder or a tweezer, only leaving the wanted design on the mat. Now remove the Transfer Tape liner. Carefully, and with the sticky side down, place it on the mat with the design. Gently press to remove any air bubbles.

Whatever surface you want the design on, it should be clean and dry. Carefully place the vinyl on the surface and gently press it down. Remove the tap by peeling it off at a 45-degree angle. If it is difficult, burnish it by using a scrapper.

How to Cut Basswood by Cricut?

For cutting a word, make sure that it is not thicker than 11 mm. Use a strong grip mat for its cutting. Handle the wood carefully, as the wood can be more fragile and easier to break. Use a craft knife and a ruler for this project. Clean the wood or use compressed air to remove all the dust. Mirror the images on Design Space. Brayer can be used to provide adhesion to the mat. Remove the white wheelers to the side of the machine. Check that the wood is not under the rollers; otherwise, it can cause damage. Make sure the design stays inside the edges of the wood — test before cutting the project.

Chapter 3 The Best Materials for Cricut

Cricut machines have been designed to handle a wide variety of materials. Most of the machines can work with a majority of materials, but they do have specialties among them. Read on for more information on the Cricut Explore One, Cricut Explore Air 2, Cricut Maker, and Cricut EasyPress 2 and the materials that work best with each.

Cricut Explore One

This machine only has one carriage, so you might find yourself swapping out tools more often than with the other machines. This machine can cut over 100 different materials. It can also write and score. Here's a sampling of some of the most common materials used with the Explore One machine.

- Vinyl – Vinyl, outdoor vinyl, glitter vinyl, metallic vinyl, matte vinyl, stencil vinyl, dry erase vinyl, chalkboard vinyl, adhesive foils, holographic vinyl, printable vinyl, vinyl transfer tape, iron-on vinyl, glitter iron-on vinyl, foil iron-on, holographic iron-on, printable iron-on for light or dark fabric, flocked iron-on vinyl, and neon iron-on vinyl

- Paper – Cardstock, glitter cardstock, pearl paper, poster board, scrapbook paper, vellum, party foil, cereal boxes, construction paper, copy paper, flat cardboard, flocked cardstock and paper, foil embossed paper, freezer paper, kraft board, kraft paper, metallic cardstock and paper, notebook paper, paper grocery bags, parchment paper, paper board, pearl cardstock and paper, photographs, mat board, rice paper, solid core cardstock, watercolor paper, and wax paper

- Fabric – Burlap, canvas, cotton, denim, duck cloth, faux leather, faux suede, felt, flannel, leather, linen, metallic leather, oilcloth, polyester, printable fabric, silk, and wool felt

- Specialty – Adhesive foil, adhesive wood, aluminum sheets, aluminum foil, balsa wood, birch wood, corkboard, corrugated paper, craft foam, duct tape, embossable foil, foil acetate, glitter foam, magnet sheets, metallic vellum, paint chips, plastic, sticker paper, shrink plastic, stencil material, tissue paper, temporary tattoo paper, transparency film, washi sheets and tape, window cling, wood veneer, and wrapping paper

Cricut Explore Air 2

The Explore Air 2 can cut the same materials as the Explore One. The difference is that it has two carriages instead of one, so it's easier to swap between tools. It's also a bit faster than the Explore One. The Air machines have wireless and Bluetooth capabilities, so you can use the Cricut Design Space on your phone, tablet, or laptop without connecting directly to the machine.

Cricut Maker

The Cricut Maker has about 10x the cutting power of the Explore machines. It includes a rotary blade and a knife blade, so in addition to all the above materials, it can cut into more robust fabrics and materials. With the sharper blades, it's also better at cutting into more delicate materials without damaging them. Here's a list of some of the additional materials the Maker can cut.

- Acrylic felt

- Bamboo fabric

- Bengaline

- Birch

- Boucle

- Broadcloth

- Burlap

- Bonded silk

- Calico

- Cambric

- Canvas

- Carbon fiber

- Cashmere

- Challis

- Chambray

- Chantilly lace

- Charmeuse satin

- Chiffon

- Chintz

- Chipboard

- Corduroy

- Crepe paper

- Cutting mat protector

- Dotted Swiss

- Double cloth

- Double knit

- Dupioni silk

- EVA foam

- Eyelet
- Faille
- Fleece
- Foulard
- Gabardine
- Gauze
- Gel sheet
- Georgette
- Gossamer
- Grois point
- Habutai
- Heather
- Heavy watercolor paper
- Homespun fabric
- Interlock knit
- Jacquard
- Jersey

- Jute
- Kevlar
- La Coste
- Lycra
- Mesh
- Metal
- Microfiber
- Moleskin
- Monk's cloth
- Muslin
- Nylon
- Organza
- Handmade paper
- Plush
- Sailcloth
- Satin silk
- Seersucker

- Sequined cloth

- Tafetta

- Tulle

- Tweed

- Velvet

- Wool crepe

Cricut EasyPress 2

The Cricut EasyPress 2 is a small, convenient heat press. It works with any type of iron-on material and can adhere to fabrics, wood, paper, and more. Cricut also offers Infusible inks that are transferred to the material using heat. The EasyPress is a great alternative to iron, as it heats more quickly and more evenly.

Crafting Blanks

The objects you decorate using your Cricut can be referred to as blanks. This can be absolutely any object, and it can be something you stick vinyl to, etch, paint, draw on, write on, or anything else you can think of. They're called blanks because they provide a mostly blank surface to be decorated, though they can also have colors or designs.

Some popular blanks are cups, mugs, wine or champagne glasses, travel mugs, tumblers, and other such drinking vessels. Craft stores will usually sell these, but you can find them at almost any store. They don't need to be considered a "craft" supply for you to use. Most stores have a selection of plain cups and mugs or travel mugs and tumblers with no designs. As long as you can imagine a Cricut project with it, it's fair game.

Drink wares aren't the only kitchen or dining-related blanks. Get creative with plates, bowls, and serving utensils. Find blank placemats or coasters at most stores. Decorate mason or other types of jars. Dry goods containers, measuring cups, food storage containers, pitchers, and jugs—anything you can put in your kitchen can serve as a great blank for your projects.

Clothing is another popular choice for Cricut projects. T-shirts are easy to make with iron-on vinyl, and you can find cheap blanks at any store or a larger selection at craft stores. In fact, craft stores will typically have a large selection of clothing blanks, such as t-shirts, long sleeve shirts, ball caps, plain white shoes, plain bags, and so on. Thrift stores or consignment shops can be an unusual option as well. You could find a shirt with an interesting pattern that you'd like to add an iron-on to or something similar.

Glass is fun to work with and has a ton of project options with your Cricut machine. Glass blocks can be found at craft or hardware stores. Many stores that carry kitchenware will have plain glass cutting boards, or you can find them online. Craft stores and home goods stores could sell glass trinkets or décor that you can decorate. You can even buy full panes of glass at your local hardware store and have them cut to your desired size.

There are plenty of blanks related to electronics as well. Electronics stores, online stores, and some craft stores offer phone and tablet case blanks. They might be clear, white or black, or colored. Portable battery packs are another option as well. Many times, these blanks are significantly cheaper than already decorated ones, or you can buy them in bulk for a lower price. Get your phone case for a cheaper price and customize it how you like.

Book covers make great blanks, as well. Customize the cover of a sketchbook, notebook, or journal. Repair the cover of an aged book. Or, create a new book cover for a plain one that you have. If you have old books that you aren't going to read, create a new fake cover for them and use them as décor.

Chapter 4 Projects on the Cricut Explore Air 2

Cutting Letters and Shapes for Scrapbooking

Shapes are one of the most vital features in Cricut Design Space. They are used for creating some of the best designs. In this tutorial, you will learn how to cut letters or texts, how to add shapes, and how to adjust the size, colors and rotate shapes.

To add a shape;

1. Log into your Design Space.

2. From the drop-down menu, click "Canvas". You will be taken to the canvas or work area.

3. Click "Shapes" on the left panel of the canvas.

4. A window will pop up with all the shapes available in Cricut Design Space.

5. Click to add shape.

We have explained the process of adding a shape. To cut a shape;

1. Click "Linetype". Linetype lets your machine know whether you plan on cutting, drawing or scoring a shape.

2. Select "Cut" as Linetype and proceed with cutting the shape.

Cutting Letters

Cutting letters or texts is simple if you know how to do it. To cut letters;

1. First of all, you need to add the text you want to cut. Click "Add Text" on the left panel of the canvas.

2. Place text in the area where you want to cut it. Highlight text and click on the slice tool. If you have multiple lines of texts, weld them and create a single layer. Then, use the slice tool.

3. Move the sliced letters from the circle and delete the ones you don't need.

How to Make Simple Handmade Cards

If you want to test your crafting skills, the Cricut Explore Air 2 has made it possible for you to be creative with designing whatever you want to design on the Design Space. We will be teaching you how to use your Cricut Explore Air 2 to make simple cards.

1. Log into Design Space with your details. Do this on your Mac/Windows PC.

2. On the left-hand side of the screen, select "Shapes". Add the square shape.

3. By default, there is no rectangular shape, so you have to make do with the square shape. However, you can adjust the length and width. You can change the shape by clicking on the padlock icon at the bottom left of the screen. Change the size and click on the padlock icon to relock it.

4. Click "Score Line" and align.

5. Create your first line. You should make it long. Use the "zoom in" option to see better if you are having difficulties with sight.

6. Select the first line you have created and duplicate. It's easier that way than creating another long line. You will see the duplicate option when you right-click on your first line.

7. Follow the same duplication process and create a third line.

8. Rotate the third line to the bottom so that it connects the other two parallel lines you earlier created. Remember to zoom in to confirm the lines are touching.

9. Duplicate another line, just like you did the other. Rotate it to the top so that it touches the two vertical parallel lines. You should have created a big rectangular shape.

10. Highlight your rectangular shape (card). Select "Group" in the upper right corner.

11. Now, change the "Score" option "cut". You can do this by clicking on the little pen icon.

12. Your lines will change from dotted to thick straight lines.

13. Select the "Attach" option at the bottom right-hand side of the screen. The four lines will be attached and will get the card ready to be cut on the mat correctly.

14. You can adjust the size of the card as you like. At this point, you can add images or texts to beautify your card anyhow you want it.

15. After you are done, select the "Make it" button and then "Continue" to cut your card out.

If you don't know how to create a style on your cards with shapes, follow these simple steps to create one.

1. Select your choice of shape. Let's choose stars, for example. Select the "Shape" option and click on the star.

2. Add two stars.

3. Select the first star and click "Flip" and then select "Flip Vertical".

4. Align both stars to overlap them at the center.

5. Select "Weld" to make a new shape and add a scoreline.

6. Align them at the center and attach them.

7. Select "Make it button" and then "Continue" to cut your card out.

If you don't know how to add text or write on a card, follow the processes below.

1. Select your choice of shape. Let's choose a hexagon, for example. Select the "Shape" option and click on the hexagon shape.

2. Use your favorite pattern.

3. Add a scoring line and rotate it.

4. Click "Add Text". A box will appear on the canvas or work area of your project. Write your desired text. Let's say you choose to write "A Star Is Born Strong" and "And Rugged" on the two hexagonal shapes. Choose the fonts and style of writing.

5. Select the first text and flip vertically or horizontally.

6. Select the second text and flip vertically. Click "Flip" and select flip vertically. Doing this will make the text not look upside down.

7. Attach Select "Make it button" and then "Continue" to cut your card out. Follow the cutting process on the screen to full effect.

How to Make a Simple T-Shirt

You can use your Cricut Explore Air 2 to make nice T-shirts designs and it's quite easy to do. Cricut cuts out an iron-on vinyl design easily and simply. I will teach you how to make a simple t-shirt with the Cricut Explore Air 2.

In this tutorial, we will be using iron-on vinyl. Iron-on vinyl is a type of vinyl, like an adhesive that will stick to any fabric when applied using an iron.

1. Log into your Design Space.

2. Select "New Project" and then click on "Templates" in the top left corner. Choosing a template makes it easier to visualize your design to know how good or bad it will be on your T-shirt.

3. Choose "Classic T-Shirt" and pick your preferred style, size, and color.

4. You will see tons of beautiful designs for iron-on T-shirts. Browse through the entire images before you make your choice.

5. Remember, if your preferred design isn't available, you can upload your pictures to the Cricut Design Space. We have created a tutorial on how to upload your own images to Cricut Design Space.

6. After you have selected the image, resize the image to fit the T-shirt. You can do this by clicking the resize handle in the bottom part of your design and dragging the mouse to enlarge or reduce.

7. When you are done, click the "Make it" button in the top right corner. You will be told to connect your Cricut machine.

8. Toggle the green "Mirror" button on. Toggling it on will make sure your design is not cut backward.

9. Face the shiny part of your vinyl design down on your cutting mat. Remember to move the smart set dial to the iron-on option.

10. Remove all the vinyl designs you don't want to be transferred to your project when it's ironed. Use your weeding tool to remove those little bits that will jeopardize your beautiful design. This process is called weeding.

11. Transfer your design to your T-shirt when you are done weeding. You can either use an iron or an EasyPress. Preheat your EasyPress before use.

12. Congrats! You just learned how to make a simple T-shirt on the Cricut Design Space.

How to Make a Leather Bracelet

The Cricut Explore Air 2 can be pretty amazing in doing a variety of things. One of those things is being able to make a leather bracelet with your Cricut. You can create pretty cool designs that you can turn into wearable pieces of jewelry.

To make a leather bracelet, you need your Cricut Explore Air 2, a deep point blade, faux leather, marker, ruler, craft knife, bracelet cut file, transfer tape, and a grip mat. You will also need glue, an EasyPress or iron and an SVG design to crown it up.

Follow these steps to create your leather bracelets.

1. Log into your Design Space account menu.

2. Select "Canvas".

3. Upload an art set from Jen Goode into the Design Space. The Jen Goode is a set of designs with 4 different image layouts.

4. Ungroup the designs and hide the layers you don't require after selecting your design.

5. Create a base cut of the shape you want to use. Use a cut file and create the shape you want. For example, you can use a shape tool to create a circular design.

6. Add circle cutouts with basic shapes. Duplicate the layer so that you will use it for the back of the bracelet.

7. Set your iron or EasyPress ready and apply the vinyl to the uppermost layer of your leather.

8. Spread a thin coat of glue on the back of the duplicated layer and press it with the other layer together.

9. Add your bracelet strap or chain together with some other ornaments.

10. Congratulations! You have just made your first leather bracelet.

Making a Stencil for Painting with the Cricut Explore Air 2

To make a stencil, you can either use the ready-made designs or make your own design. This tutorial will be based on how to create a stencil for painting.

1. Log in to your Design Space.

2. Click "Canvas" from the drop-down menu.

3. Click "Add Text".

4. Highlight text and change to your preferred font.

5. All your letters must be separated. If they aren't, click the ungroup button to separate. The letters must overlap. This will allow you to drag each letter as you please.

6. Arrange your text line as you want it. If you notice each letter is still showing individually, highlight the text box and click "Weld" at the bottom right of the panel.

7. Click "Attach". Make sure the text is highlighted. This will make the letters arranged properly when it goes to the cut mat.

8. Your stencil design is ready!

Making a Vinyl Sticker

First of all, you need to have an idea of the vinyl sticker that you want. Get ideas online or from forums. Once you have gotten the picture, make a sketch of it to see how the sticker would look. After you have done this, follow the steps below;

1. Use an image editing software like Photoshop or Illustrator. Design to your taste and save. Make sure you know the folder it is saved to.

2. Now, open your Design Space.

3. Click "New Project".

4. Scroll to the bottom left-hand side and click "Upload".

5. Drag and drop the design you created with your photo editing app.

6. Select your image type. If you want to keep your design simple, select simple.

7. Select which area of the image is not part of it.

8. Before you forge ahead, select the image as cut to have a preview. You can go back if there is a need for adjustments.

9. Select "Cut".

10. Weed excess vinyl.

11. Use a transfer tape on top of the vinyl. This will make the vinyl stay in position.

12. Go over the tape and ensure all the bibles are nowhere to be found.

13. Peel away the transfer tape and you have your vinyl sticker.

Chapter 5 Making Money with Cricut

It is a well-known fact in the world of business that to make money, you first need to invest money. With that being said, if you already own a "Cricut" cutting machine, then you can jump to the next paragraph, but if you are debating if it's worth the investment, then read on. As mentioned earlier, "Cricut" has a range of cutting machines with distinctive capabilities offered at a varying price range. The "Cricut Explore Air 2" is priced at $249.99, and the "Cricut Maker" is priced at $399.99 (the older "Cricut Explore Air" model may be available for sale on Amazon at a cheaper price).

Now, if you were to buy any of these machines during a holiday sale with a bundle deal that comes with a variety of tools, accessories, and materials for a practice project as well as free trial membership to "Cricut Access", you would already be saving enough to justify the purchase for your personal usage. The cherry on top would be if you can use this investment to make more money. You can always get additional supplies in a bundle deal or from your local stores at a much cheaper price. All in all, those upfront costs can easily be justified with the expenses you budget for school projects that require you to cut letters and shapes, creating personalized gifts for your loved ones or decorating your home with customized decals, and of course, your own jewelry creations. These are only a handful of the reasons to buy a "Cricut" machine for your personal use.

Let's start scraping the mountain of "Cricut" created wealth to help you get rich while enjoying your work!

At this stage, let's assume that you have bought a "Cricut" cutting machine and have enough practice with beginner-friendly projects. You now have the skillset and the tools to start making money with your "Cricut" machine, so let's jump into how you can make it happen. The ways listed below have been tried and tested as successful money-making strategies that you can implement with no hesitations.

1. Selling Pre-Cut Customized Vinyl

Vinyl is a super beginner-friendly material to work with and comes in a variety of colors and patterns to add to its great reputation. You can create custom labels for glass containers and jars to help anyone who wants to organize their pantry. Explore the online trends and adjust the labels. Once you have your labels designed, the easiest approach is to set up an "Etsy" shop, which is free and very easy to use. It's almost like opening an Amazon prime membership account. If your design is in demand, you will have people ordering even with no advertising. But if you would like to keep the tempo high, then advertise your "Etsy" listing on "Pinterest" and other social media platforms. This is a sure way to generate more traffic to your "Etsy" store and convert potential customers into paying customers. An important note here is the pictures being used on your listing.

You cannot use any of the stock images from the "Design Space" application and must use your own pictures that match the product you are selling.

Create a package of 5 or 6 different labels like sugar, salt, rice, oats, beans, etc., that can be sold as a standard packager and offer a customized package that will allow the customer to request any word that they need to be included in their set. Since these labels weigh next to nothing, shipping can easily be managed with standard mail with usually only a single postage stamp, depending on the delivery address. Make sure you do not claim the next day or two-day delivery for these. Build enough delivery time so you can create and ship the labels without any stress. Once you have an established business model, you can adjust the price and shipping of your product, but more on that later. Check out other "Etsy" listings to make sure your product pricing is competitive enough and you are attracting enough potential buyers.

Now, once you have traction in the market, you can offer additional vinyl-based projects like bumper stickers, iron-on, or heat transfer vinyl designs that people can transfer on their clothing using a standard heating iron. Really, once you have gained some clientele, you can modify and customize all your listings to develop into a one-stop-shop for all things vinyl (a great name for your future Etsy shop, right!).

2. Selling Finished Pieces

You would be using your "Cricut" machines for a variety of personal projects like home décor, holiday décor, personalized clothing, and more. Next time you embark on another one of your creative journeys leading to unique creations, just make two of everything, and you can easily put the other product to sell on your "Etsy" shop. Another great advantage is that you will be able to save all your projects on the "Design Space" application for future use, so if one of your projects goes viral, you can easily buy the supplies and turn them into money-making offerings. This way, not only your original idea for personal usage will be paid off, but you can make much more money than you invested in it, to begin with.

Again, spend some time researching what kind of designs and decorations are trending in the market and use them to spark up inspiration for your next project. Some of the current market trends include customized cake and cupcake toppers and watercolor designs that can be framed as fancy wall decorations. The cake toppers can be made with cardstock, which is another beginner-friendly material, light in weight, and can be economically shipped tucked inside an envelope.

3. Personalized Clothing and Accessories

T-shirts with cool designs and phrases are all the rage right now. Just follow a similar approach to the selling vinyl section and take it up a notch. You can create sample clothing with an iron-on design and market it with "can be customized further at no extra charge" or "transfer the design on your own clothing" to get traction in the market. You can buy sling bags and customize them with unique designs to be sold as finished products at a higher price than a plain boring sling bag.

Consider creating a line of products with a centralized theme like the DC Marvel characters or the "Harry Potter" movies and design custom t-shirts, hats, and even bodysuits for babies. You can create customized party favor boxes and gift bags at the request of the customer. Once your product has a dedicated customer base, you can get project ideas from them directly and quote them a price for your work. Isn't that great?!?!

Another big advantage of the heat transfer vinyl, as mentioned earlier, is that anyone can transfer the design on their desired item of clothing using a standard household iron. But you would need to include the transfer instructions with the order letting them know exactly how to prep for the heat transfer without damaging their chosen clothing item. And again, heat transfer vinyl can be easily shipped using a standard mailing envelope.

4. Marketing on Social Media

We are all aware of how social media has become a marketing platform for not only established corporations but also small businesses and budding entrepreneurs. Simply add hashtags like for sale, product, selling, free shipping, the sample included, and more to entice potential buyers. Join "Facebook" community pages and groups for handcraft sellers and buyers to market your products. Use catchy phrases like customization available at no extra cost or free returns if not satisfied when posting the products on these pages as well as your personal "Facebook" page. Use "Twitter" to share feedback from your happy customers to widen your customer base. You can do this by creating a satisfaction survey that you can email to your buyers or include a link to your "Etsy" listing, asking for online reviews and ratings from your customers.

Another tip here is to post pictures of anything and everything you have created using "Cricut" machines, even those that you did not plan to sell. You never know who else might need something that you deemed unsellable. Since you will be creating these only after the order has been placed, you can easily gather the required supplies after the fact and get crafting.

5. Target Local Farmer's Market and Boutiques

If you like the thrill of a show-and-tell, then reserve a booth at a local farmer's market and show up with some ready-to-sell crafts. In this case, you are relying on the number of people attending and a subset of those who might be interested in making a purchase from you. If you are in an urban neighborhood where people are keenly interested in unique art designs but do not have the time to create them on their own, you can easily make big bucks by setting a decent price point for your products.

Bring flyers to hand out to people so they can reach you through one of your social media accounts or email and check all your existing "Etsy" listings. Think of these events as a means of marketing for those who are not as active online but can be excited with customized products to meet their next big life events, such as a baby shower, birthday party, or wedding.

One downside to participating in local events is the generation of mass inventory and booth displays, topped with expenses to load and transport the inventory. You may or may not be able to sell all of the inventory depending on the size of the event, but as I said earlier, you can still make the most of this by marketing your products and building up a local clientele.

50+ Business Ideas You Can Make with Your Cricut and Sell

- Wall art canvas

- Leather bracelet

- Frosty wreath

- Iron-on T-shirt

- Customized tools

- Customized cutting board

- Customized kitchen towels

- Customized lanyards

- Doormats

- Rustic signs

- Coffee mugs

- Holiday bucket

- Customized plates

- Pillows case

- Bedsheets

- Paper succulent

- Planner stickers

- Sports cuff

- Key chains

- Wooden signs

- Monogrammed ornament

- Blankets

- Laptop cases

- Monogrammed pillows

- Car stickers
- Home decals
- Christmas greeting cards
- Interior designs
- Pet tags
- Cake tops
- Scrapbook pages
- Gift boxes
- Addressed envelopes
- Felt coasters
- Customized tote bags
- Flower bouquets
- Monogrammed water bottle
- Model decals
- Paper pennants
- Metallic tags

- Paper peonies
- Santa sacks
- Christmas advent calendar
- Paper heart box
- Paper tulips
- Magnolia blossom
- Gift card holder
- Paper flower lanterns
- Paper purse
- Paper poppers
- Halloween buddies
- Paper fiery house and more

Chapter 6 Helpful Troubleshooting Techniques

Problems with Printing Images

The Explore machine will work with a variety of printers, but some printers will jam when using card stock. The best option is to use a printer that feeds the card stock from the rear. The fewer turns the card stock makes in the printer, the less chance of it jamming.

Play it safe and don't use a laser printer for vinyl or sticky material. The heat of the printer will melt the material and could damage the printer.

Design Space has a printable area that is 6.75 by 9.25. This is a lot bigger than past versions.

When you're working with an image you're going to print, select a square from the Shapes tool and place it behind your image. Make the size of the square 6.75 and 9.25. Then you can clearly see while you're working with your image whether or not it is within the printable area. Make the square a light color so you can see it separate from your image.

You can put more than one image in the box. Attach the images so you can move them all at one time. Delete the box before printing.

It's easier than ever to create custom designs for multiple uses by changing their Line type instead of redesigning the whole project.

Pens

When you're inserting a pen into your machine, place a piece of scrap paper under the pen. This keeps the pen from marking up your material or the machine when you click it into the clamp.

There are several ways to breathe new life into dried markers, sometimes it is enough to soak the tip or fill the marker with 90% alcohol.

Problems with Cutting Images

Before unloading the mat, try to determine if the material has been cut to satisfaction. If not, manually hit the cut button on the Explore and cut it again several times.

Use the Custom Material Settings in Design Space to increase or decrease the pressure, add multiple cuts, choose an intricate cut setting, or change materials. Within each category, there are several listings for different kinds of paper or card stock, for example. Just try selecting a different kind and see if that helps.

Tip: Create your own custom settings for any material by selecting Manage Custom Materials from the main menu. Then just click Add New Material and enter the information.

Some complex designs won't cut well in Fast Mode so just cut it regularly. Make sure the blade and mat are clean.

If your images are not cutting correctly, be sure and wipe the mat and scrape off any access material left from previous projects. If the mat is severely scored or gouged, replace it.

Try switching to another mat, such as the stickier blue mat. If the mat isn't sticky enough, the material can slip and won't cut properly. Or tape the paper to the mat.

Then carefully clean the blade. If there is still a problem, it might be time to replace the blade. Using the new German Carbide blade is your best option for optimal cutting. Believe it or not, there can be a slight difference in the cutting edge between one new blade and another.

Make sure the blade fits tightly in the housing. Regularly clean out the blade housing of fibers that accumulate and interfere with the cutting process. Blow on the housing or use a straightened paper clip and carefully loosen the glued material.

Since the angle of the deep cutting blade is different, try using it on regular material when experiencing problems.

If you get a message saying that the image is too large, you simply need to resize the image to make it smaller. Some people think that since the mat is 12 x 12 they can use 12 x 12 images. But there is a slight space left for margins, so the largest image size is 11.5 x 11.5. You can purchase a 12 x 24 mat to make larger cuts of 11.5 x 23.5.

If all else fails, try a different material. Some users find that certain brands of paper or card stock work better than others.

Mats

If your mat is too sticky when it's new, place a white T-shirt on it and press lightly or just pat it with your hands. This will reduce some of the stickiness.

When using a brayer and thin paper, don't apply a lot of pressure on the mat. This makes it hard to remove without ripping the paper.

Always clean your mat after each use. Use a scraper to remove small bits of lint or paper that have been left behind. These small scraps will cause problems with future projects.

You can wipe the mat with a damp cloth. Then replace the plastic cover between uses to prevent dust and dirt from sticking to the mat.

When the mat has lost its stickiness, tape the material to the mat around the edges or wash it with a little soap and water, rinse, let dry and it's good to go.

Have you seen those food-grade flexible cutting mats or boards? Some users are turning them into Cricut mats. Look for the thin plastic ones that are 12 x 12 or 12 x 24.

Use spray adhesive and cover the mat leaving a border so the glue doesn't get on the rollers or just spray the back of the card stock to adhere to the makeshift mat.

Load and Unload

When you load the mat into the Explore, always make sure that it's up against the roller wheels and under the guides. This assures the material will load straight when you press the load button.

When the cut is complete, never pull the mat out of the machine, as this can damage the wheels. Always hit the unload button and then remove the mat.

To extend the life of the mat, turn it around and load it from the bottom edge. Position the images on different parts of the mat instead of always cutting in the upper left corner.

Curling

Here's how to avoid curling material into a useless mess. When working with new mats, they tend to hold on for dear life.

When you're pulling a project off the mat, do not pull the paper (or whatever material) up and away from the mat. This will cause it to curl into a mess.

Instead, turn the mat over and curl it downward. Pull the mat away from the paper instead of pulling the paper up and away from the mat.

It seems like a slight difference, but it will save you from trying to uncurl and flatten a project. Just remember how curled the mat was when you first unboxed it had to wait till it flattened out.

Blades

When cutting adhesive material, glue accumulates on the blades and should be periodically removed. Dip a Q-Tip in nail polish remover to clean any sticky residue build-up. Check the cutting edge for nicks and that the tip is still intact.

Note: These blades are extremely sharp. Always use the utmost care when removing them or replacing them in your Cricut. Never leave them lying within reach of children. Save the tips and cap the blades before trashing them.

For best results, use the German Carbide blades. The regular Cricut blades will fit in the Explore blade housing even though they're shaped differently.

At this time there is no German Carbide deep cut blade for the Explore. The blade that comes with the deep-cut housing for the Explore is the regular deep-cutting blade.

Materials

When planning a project with new material, it's good to do a small test first to make sure the material cuts the way you want. This will save you from potential problems and from wasting a large amount of material.

Try one of the in-between settings on the Smart Set Dial. Some card stock is thicker than other types, so you may need to adjust settings, use the multi-cut settings or re-cut the image manually by hitting the cut button again.

By default, the Smart Set dial for paper, vinyl, iron-on, card stock, fabric, poster board has been set up to work best with Cricut products. Each material has three settings on the dial. If the cuts aren't deep enough, increase the pressure or decrease the pressure if the cuts are too deep. For even more control, use the custom settings within Design Space.

Additionally, using a deep cutting blade (with the housing) or adjusting the stickiness of the mat may help.

Iron-on Vinyl

Sometimes the iron-on vinyl sticks to the iron. First, be sure your iron is not too hot. Follow the recommendations on the product. Make sure you purchased the type of vinyl that can be applied with an iron and not a professional heat press.

Next, try using parchment paper, Teflon sheet or a piece of cotton fabric between the vinyl and the iron. Use a firm heat-resistant surface such as a ceramic tile or wooden cutting board to place your project on. Press and hold instead of ironing back and forth.

Always flip the image in Design Space. Put the vinyl's shiny side down while cutting and the shiny side up when attaching to the material.

Iron-on Glitter Vinyl

When working with glitter vinyl, I move the dial one notch to move the iron-on vinyl onto the clear card stock. It seems to cut better using that setting.

After you make the first cut, do not remove the mat from the machine. Check to see if it has cut the vinyl. Sometimes I have to run it one more time for the cut to be complete. Especially if it is a new brand that I have not worked with.

Stencils

There are many materials you can use to make stencils. Some users suggested plastic file folders that can be found cheaply at a Dollar Store. Another option is sending laminating sheets through a laminating machine and then putting them through your Cricut to cut the stencil. Run it through twice to make sure cuts are complete.

Problems with Machine Pausing

If your Cricut machine stops while cutting, writing or scoring, I've already made several suggestions to correct the problem, here's another option.

It may be the project itself, if it always happens, try deleting that project and recreating it. Turn off your computer and disconnect from your machine. Turn off your Cricut machine and wait a few moments. Then restart and reconnect.

Problems with Bluetooth Wireless

If you're using an Explore Air or Explore Air 2, your Cricut machine is already Bluetooth enabled. But with an Explore or Explore One you will need to buy a Bluetooth adaptor.

Make sure your machine is close when using Bluetooth, no more than 15 feet from the computer.

Make sure to verify your computer is Bluetooth enabled. If not, you'll need to buy a Bluetooth Dongle and place it in an unused USB port.

If you lose the Bluetooth connection, try uninstalling your Cricut under Bluetooth devices and then reinstalling.

Some people find their Design Space software works faster using the USB cord instead of the Bluetooth connection.

Chapter 7 Hacks, Tips, and Techniques

Hacks, tips, and techniques—call it what you want, but every Cricut crafter needs to know them to make crafting much easier, faster, and fuss-free. We explore the many hacks regarding tools and supplies organizing, how to get the most out of your purchases, how to save time and money, and much more.

How to Organize Cricut Supplies

Making your craft space organized, no matter how big or small is imperative. First things firsts:

Cricut Mat Organization

You will have plenty of mats for various crafting needs and the more you continue your Cricut crafts, the more mats you'll have. So how do you keep them all organized? Hanging your mats on the wall according to the grip strength is one way. You can use basket storage or file storage, and you can even use command hooks to organize and sort your mats. Having them displayed on the wall will save you some time looking and searching for them.

Cricut Vinyl Rolls

One of the best ways to keep all your vinyl rolls perfectly organized is by using Ikea trash bag holders. Crafters swear by it. Just do a quick Google search, and you'll find plenty of images showing you how you can stack these rolls easily in the holders. The holders cost only about $10 or so, and they can hold up to 14 rolls each. Get a few of them and organize your rolls according to color and style.

Cricut Tools

For tools, you can use jars or canisters to keep your tools safely and securely. Some crafters also use $5 pegboards purchased from Target that have tiny holes in them that you can easily hang. Keeping them on pegboards prevents the nuisance of digging around for them. You get to see your tools displayed nicely and there's no guessing where everything is. All your tools are within easy reach.

How to Quickly Weed Vinyl

Weeding is both satisfying and troublesome at the same time. Some crafters find joy in weeding out all the little cuts because it's very satisfying to see your artwork coming together, but it is bothersome as well because weeding out takes time.

The best way to make this process fast is by using your Cricut Bright Pad. All you need to do is place your craft on the top of the lightbox, so the light peeks through all those intricate cut lines. You can see all these lines more visibly, and it also saves time because you do not need to guess where the cuts are. If the BrightPad is not within your budget, you can also place your vinyl on a window or a brighter area, so the light makes it easier for you to see.

Charge Your Electronics from Your Cricut Maker

Make use of the USB port on the side to power up your phone or your laptop or tablet or even your BrightPad. Newer versions of the Cricut Machine come with a space that enables you to prop your phone or tablet. Did you know that? Now you do.

How to Use a Cricut Easy Press for Perfect Results

If you are doing iron-on projects, you'll save yourself a lot of time and frustration by investing in the Easy Press from Cricut. While iron-ons are meant to be ironed on with your conventional iron, you'll notice that there is a major difference between using an iron and using the Easy Press.

Conventional irons have hot and cold spots that result in you taking more time to cover the surface of your iron projects to ensure that everything sticks on easily. But with the Easy Press, you have a large surface area and the heat is evenly distributed over the entire surface, ensuring that your iron is ironed safely. You do not need to worry about burning your project because the temperature is too hot on one end while the other end doesn't even stick. When working with iron-ons, look at the Cricut temperature chart to select the temperature that is appropriate for your craft and the time needed to press until the machine beeps.

How to Use Vinyl Scraps

Many crafters do not throw away their vinyl scraps because they can be used again. Plus, it helps if you use the scraps again to save the environment. One of the best ways to use scraps is to place them on your mat and use the Snap Mat feature found in the Cricut App. What this does is that it will take a photo of your mat and allow you to arrange your designs on the scraps so that they can be cut out perfectly. This means no more guesswork and no more waste. These scraps also work great with quilters working on fussy cuts on their fabric. You can use the Snap Mat features to take a photo of the fabric and the mat. Next, place these designs over the images you want to cut out.

How to Clean a Cricut Mat

Cricut machine, there are many ways to clean it depending on how dirty your machine is and how often you use it. Sometimes it also depends on the materials you use that make your machine dirty. For example, using felt means you'd need to grab stray pieces using tweezers. Another great way to clean your Cricut machine is to use a lint roller across the entire machine to pick up debris, scrap vinyl, and pieces of felt. You can also use this roller on your mats.

To clean your mats, if there are any leftover residue on your mats, the general rule is to use bleach and alcohol-free baby wipes to gently wipe the mat clean and remove it from grime, glue, and dust. You can also get yourself GOO GONE. Spray this on your mat and let it sit for 15 minutes, then use a scraper tool to remove the adhesive. But do this only if your mat is very dirty. Otherwise, wet wipes will do.

Another tip to keep your mats clean is by putting a protective cover back over them when you are not using them.

If you want to clean your mats based on their stickiness, here is what you can do:

Cleaning the Pink FabricGrip Mats

The pink mats are slightly tricky to keep clean. Here's what you can do:

- Do not touch the adhesive side at all because oils from your fingers can affect the carpet adhesive.

- Never use the scraper on your fabric mat, as you may end up removing the adhesive too.

- Instead, use the Cricut spatula or tweezers as well as the Cricut Strong Grip transfer tape to clean your mats.

- Never use any cleaning agent or soap and water on your fabric mat.

- If you end up getting fuzzy materials like fleece and felt on your mat, use transfer tape behind your fabric before sticking it to the mat. This will prevent the fuzz from getting onto your mat.

The great thing about the pink FabricGrip mat is that it will not lose its stickiness over time, even when there's leftover fiber from your previous projects. The rotary blade will continue cutting right through them.

Chapter 8 Tips and Tricks, You Need to Know to Make Cricut Machine Much Easier and Efficient

Harbor Freight is a Good Resource

Harbor Freight has sets of hooks that are similar to the weeding tool that Cricut has to offer. These sets of weeding hooks generally run very cheap and so the job just as well as Cricut's proprietary weeding hooks. If you find that this is a tool you use a lot of need to replace often, consider looking at Harbor Freight or another hardware retailer for a suitable replacement on a budget and in bulk!

Start Small

You can't purchase a Cricut machine today and start cutting wood tomorrow. Even if you're planning on using your Cricut machine for the most complicated projects, you should start small and use small projects to practice first.

Get Used to Design Space

Once you open your account on Design Space, use this guide to get conversant with all the panels and icons. Then, start with small and straightforward designs before you move to the more complicated ones.

Constantly Maintain the Machine

Not just the device, but the accessories as well. If you want them to last for a very long time, then you have to handle them with care.

Don't Limit Yourself

The great thing about Cricut is that it provides you with limitless opportunities and an excellent machine that helps you bring your designs to life. Don't limit yourself when you design with Cricut. Instead, go as far as your mind can take you.

Use Synchronized Colors to Save Time and Money

This is a great tool when you have designs that are either a composite of multiple images or inherently contain different hues of the same color. Instead of using 5 different shades of the same color, you can synchronize the colors so that you need to use only one colored sheet. To do this, simply click on the "Color Sync" tab on the "Layers Panel" on the top right corner of the screen. Then drag and drop desired layer(s) of the design to your target color layer and the moved layer will immediately be modified to have the same color as the target color.

Use the "Hide" Tool to Selectively Cut Images from the Canvas

When you want to turn your imagination into a work of art, you may want to look at and be inspired by multiple images as you work on your design. But once you get your desired design, you don't want to cut all the other images from your canvas. This is where the "Hide" tool comes in handy, so you do not need to delete the images on the Canvas to avoid cutting them along with your project design. To hide the image, you just need to click on the "eye" symbol next to those specific image layers on the "Layers Panel". The hidden images will not be deleted from the Canvas but would not appear on the cutting mat when you click the "Make It" button to cut your project.

The Power of the "Pattern" Tool

"Personalized Fridge Magnets", you can use your own uploaded images to be used as pattern fill for your designs. Moreover, you will also be able to edit the image pattern and the patterns that already exist within the "Design Space" application to create your own unique and customized patterns. The "Edit Pattern" window allows you to adjust the resolution and positioning of the pattern on your design and much more. (Remember, to use the "Pattern" feature you must use the "Print then Cut" approach for your project, with access to a printer).

Utilize the Standard "Keyboard Shortcuts"

The "Design Space" application does have all the necessary tools and to allow you to edit the images and fonts, but if you prefer to use your keyboard shortcuts to quickly edit the image, the "Design Space" application will support that. Some of the keyboard shortcuts you can use include: "Copy (Control + C)"; "Paste (Control + V)"; "Delete (Delete key)"; "Copy (Control + Z)".

Change the Position of the Design on the Cutting Mat

When you are ready to cut your design and click on the "Make It" button, you will notice that your design will be aligned on the top left corner of the mat. Now, if you are using material that was previously cut at its top left corner, you can simply drag and move the image on the "Design Space" mat to meet the positioning of your cutting material. You will be able to cut the image anywhere on the mat by moving the design to that specific position on the mat.

Moving Design from One Mat to the Another

Yes! You can not only move the design over the mat itself, but you can also move the design from one mat to another by simply clicking on the three dots (…) on top of the mat and select "Move to another mat". You will then view a pop-up window where you can select from the existing mats for your project to be used as the new mat for your selected design.

Save Cut Materials as Favorites for Quick Access

Instead of spending time filtering and searching for your cut material on the "Design Space" application over and over, just save your frequently used material by clicking on the star next to the "Cricut" logo on the "Design Space" application to save them under the "Favorites" tab next to the default "All Materials" tab.

You Can Store the Most Frequently Used Cut Materials on the "Cricut Maker"

Unlike the "Cricut Explore" series, which has dial settings for a variety of commonly used cut materials, the "Cricut Maker" requires you to use a "Custom Materials" menu within the "Design Space" application that can be accessed using the button on the machine bearing "Cricut" logo, since there is no dial to choose the material you want to cut.

Choose to Repeat the Cut of the Same Mat or Skip a Mat from Being Cut Altogether

By following the instructions on the "Design Space" and feeding the right color and size of the material to the machine, you will be able to get your design perfectly cut. You can change the order in which the mats are cut, repeat the cut of your desired mat and even skip cutting a mat if needed. You can do this easily by simply clicking on and selecting the mat you would like to cut.

You Can Edit the Cut Settings of Your Materials

You might notice that even when you have selected the default settings to cut the desired material, the material may not cut as desired. To help with this, "Design Space" allows you to adjust the cut settings for all the materials, such as the depth of the cut, the cutting blade and the number of the passes to be made by the "Cricut" device. Since this may not be as intuitive to most beginners, here's a step-by-step walkthrough of this process:

Clean Your Cutting Mat

If you want to prolong the life of your cutting mats, it is important to clean them from time to time (if not after every use). You can clean the mat with baby wipes or use other wet wipes that are alcohol-free and unscented. This will ensure that cardboard and vinyl residue and other materials do not accumulate and that dust and lint do not build up.

Carefully Remove the Materials Off the Cutting Mat

It is highly recommended to use appropriate tools to remove the material from the mat. But it is equally important to pay attention to how you are peeling the design from the mat. To prevent the material from getting damaged, it is better to peel the mat away from the design by turning the mat upside down and bending a corner of the material. Then you can slip in the spatula to remove the project easily and with no damage.

IKEA Grocery Bag Holders as Material Organizers

You will find that IKEA's grocery bag holders/dispensers are designed in such a way that they will beautifully hold several rolls of Cricut materials each! These cost only $2.99 each at IKEA, are safe for your walls, and will keep your materials aesthetically displayed while keeping them safe from wrinkling, crinkling, or worse!

No matter how cluttered your desk space gets, those rolls will always be perfectly safe up there on the wall!

Pegboard Tool Storage

You will notice that one of the more handy features of the proprietary tools that Cricut offers is that they all have little holes on the ends of their handles! This makes them perfect candidates for pegboard storage! I'm sure the brilliant minds at Cricut know this and have anticipated it.

Simply hanging a pegboard over your workspace can keep all your tools readily available, but it can also help prolong the life of your tools! Keeping your tools in a box that gets moved regularly can cause the tools to bump into each other, dulling their points or chipping their handles. Hanging your tools above your workstation ensures you'll be able to find what you need at all times, your tools will stay pristine for longer, and you'll be able to look at your pretty tools at all times!

Remove Debris with a Lint Roller

This one sounds obvious, but it's a lifesaver. Taking a lint roller to your Cricut mats can save you a lot of trouble and can keep the grip strong on your mats. Over time, you will find that paper and fabric fibers, glitter, dust, and debris get stuck to the grip on your mats. This torpedo the grip strength in no time flat!

This works with lint rollers from the dollar store or the dollar section at Target, so don't feel like you need to go above and beyond for this tip!

Wash Your Mats with Warm Water and a Mild Soap

Since Cricut strongly urges against cleaning your mats, it is imperative that you realize that you do this at your own risk. However, a large number of Cricut crafters have said that this little tip has saved them from having to buy a new mat for an extra couple of weeks, at least.

Since this is against Cricut's suggestion, it is important that you hold off on trying it until it seems like your mat may be near the end of its grip life, when you would be replacing it anyway. This is so that if you find these hacks don't work, or they do damage, you will have needed to buy a new one soon anyway!

Chapter 9 Things to Know About Cricut

Cricut Comparisons - Which to Buy?

There are currently 5 Cricut machine versions. They're made by the Provo Craft business. How can you know which to purchase? In the event, you begin small or move large off the bat? I will offer you the details of everyone in easy terms so you can create your own choice on what is right for you. We will discuss the 4 primary machines. There's currently a Cricut Cake system, but it's so much like this Cricut Expression, I am not likely to pay that you especially.

Let us Split down it...

Original Cricut: (aka Baby Bug)

- Mat dimensions = 6 x 12

- Could utilize all cartridges

- Can utilize all of blades and housings

- Can utilize markers

- Cuts any size newspaper that suits the mat

- Makes cuts that range from 1 inch to 5-1/2 inches in dimension, in half-inch increments.

- Could connect to a PC and use Design Studio or Certainly Cuts lots Computer Software

Cricut Produce

Type of a hybrid of this Baby Bug and also the saying. It's still modest but includes a number of the qualities of this Cricut Expression.

- May utilize all cartridges

- May utilize all of blade and housings

- May utilize markers

- Cuts any size newspaper that suits around the mat

- Makes cuts that range from 1/4 inch into 11-1/2 inches in dimension, in quarter-inch increments.

- Can link to a PC and use Design Studio or Positive Cuts lots Computer Software

- Innovative attribute buttons available (invert, fit to page, match to span, center stage, etc.)

- Can link to a PC and use Design Studio or Positive Cuts lots Computer Software

Cricut Length

- Mat dimensions = 12 x 12, or 12 x 24

- Could utilize all cartridges

- Can utilize all of blades and housings

- Could utilize markers

- Cut any size newspaper that is suitable for a size pad

- Makes cuts out of 1/4 inch into 23-1/2 inches in dimension, in quarter-inch increments.

- Has lots of innovative attribute buttons (reverse, fit to page, match to span, center stage, etc.)

- Has style keys (amount, autoload, portrait, etc.)

- Could link to a PC and work with Design Studio or Certain Cuts lots Computer Software.

Cricut Picture

Newest and greatest version. The design of this Cricut machine using a color printer.

- Mat dimensions = 12 x 12 (unique Dark mat)

- May utilize all cartridges

- Can utilize all of blades and housings

- Cuts or eyeglasses or equally on any size document that suits on the mat

- Makes cuts out of 1/4 inch into 11-1/2 inches in dimension, in quarter-inch increments

- Has lots of imaginative attributes (turn, fit on a page, match to span, center point, etc.)

- Has manners (amount, auto match, portrait, etc.)

- The device will print the picture and then cut it.

- Comes with an LCD display and runs on the stylus for browsing the display

- The same accessories are compatible with machines. The cartridges blades, tools and markers aren't machine-specific. The cutting pads are the sole thing that changes based upon the machine. The new Picture also needs the new mat. The aged green mats won't work with this.

If you want this system for portability, size and weight may be a variable for you.

Weight Dimensions

Private Cricut 7 lb 15.5" x 7" x 7"

Cricut Produce 10.75 lb 15.5" x 7" x 7"

Cricut Expression 13.4 lb 21.5" x 7" x 7.75"

Cricut Picture 28 lb 23.5" x 9" x13.5"

Personal and produce are equally small, mobile lightweight machines. If you're taking your endeavors to plants or distinct tasks, then you may wish to think about one of these. They're lightweight and easy to go around. The Expression is a lot heavier and bigger. In case you have a craft area or scrapbooking room and don't have to move it frequently, you have many more options with this system.

Cricut Accessories for Scrapbooking

When in regards to scrapbooking, the ideal accessories will make all of the difference. That is the reason it is a fantastic concept to select Cricut accessories for the scrapbook needs so you know that you're receiving quality scrapbooking items that you may depend on.

When you would like assistance with your scrapbooking, then Cricut is a title you can rely on to supply you with quality tools and accessories that will assist you to make good scrapbooking. By way of instance, you may take your topics and thoughts and make them a reality in ways you wouldn't have been able to do before.

You could be as imaginative as you desire. If you do not believe you are a really artistic or creative individual, you may make use of these tools to produce things that you would never have been in a position to consider earlier. If you're creative, then you are able to take that imagination even further using all the resources which Cricut can provide for you.

You can make use of these resources to your benefit to make a number of the greatest scrapbooks about. Your thoughts can become a fact, so it's going to be easier than ever before to capture those pictures and mementos coordinated into scrapbooks that you cherish forever.

When deciding on those accessories, create a record of the ones you want and desire the most. Then go back in order starting with the ones you want the most and working your way down to the ones you would like to have as you can afford them. Then you're able to buy these one or 2 at a time before your group is complete and you've got each the excellent Cricut accessories that you need on your scrapbook sets.

Here are merely a couple of those safest accessories out there:

- Deep Cut Blades
- Cricut Stamp Refill
- Cricut Jukebox
- Cricut Cartridge Storage Box
- Cricut Color Fashion
- Cricut Cutting Mats

- Cricut Spatula Tool

Now that you learn more about picking Cricut accessories such as scrapbooking, then you are able to apply this in your personal scrapbooking. You may discover that it makes your scrapbooking much simpler, and it also provides you with more layouts and more ways to utilize your imagination for exceptional scrapbooking.

Cricut Expression - Worth the Money

The Cricut Expression is selling like hot cakes on the web! What is all of the fuss about? Here I shall provide you a fast collection of the very best characteristics and enable you to determine if the Cricut filler actually cuts!

- The Cricut Expression is a really sophisticated crafting device, compared to Cricut Create along with also the Cricut Personal Electronic Cutter. The very first thing that strikes you is just how large this new version is, about its dimensions.

- It's been fabricated by a group of seasoned specialists with the only purpose of cutting letters, letters, and contours in appropriate sizes throughout the use of this 12 inches x 24 inches cutting mat.

- This superb electronic model may perform different kinds of paper clippings such as vellum and maybe even vinyl. Crafters can cut paper to little .25 inch bits and around 12 inches x 24 inches.

Cricut Explore Air 2

- Different layouts with a vast assortment of contours can be drawn up via this complex device.

- It's packed with unique attributes like Plantin faculty publication font and Accent Critical type capsules, inclusive of this 12 x 12 mat for cutting functions.

- Cricut certainly made Expression with teachers and schools in your mind. This system could be popular set up in the course space, there is little doubt about this!

- The most recent model generates an impressively high number of distinct paper cuts. But, crafters considering forming dices measuring less than 5 1/2 inches may nevertheless elect for your Cricut.

- The most important drawback could be that many crafters discover that it's tricky to produce sufficient space for the setup of the outer machine, because of the bulky casing.

- In addition to the core attributes, you get welcome bonuses such as Vehicle Load, Mix'n Match, Fit to Page, Flip and Fit to Style, etc. This updated model can be packed with all the Accent Cartridge that will surely develop the attribute of scrapbook designs.

- Together with the awesome Flip choice, you are able to track the image or chart by changing its instructions. This is much more entertaining than it seems!

- The center point process is a real-time saver. It helps users to place the blade over the authentic center indicating this photograph or picture, then trims the particular place on the photograph for you - really convenient.

- The multi-cut mechanism allows the unit to reduce thick-sized chipboard considerably deeper than previously.

- The Line spin placing helps you to fix the blade into another line when performing heavy cuts.

- Additionally the Mat Size program will permit the user to place 12 inches x 24 inches or 12 inches x 12 inches.

Cricut Design Studio Help for Newbies - 5 Minutes Tutorial!

Switch on your PC! If you have successfully set up your Cricut Design Studio applications, you need to observe the tiny green Cricut Bug appearing at you with large eyes directly out of your desktop computer.

When you load the program, you are going to be shown a huge window with elements that may appear odd (or not so odd) at first glance.

Here is a brief description of the chief things in the Cricut Design Studio applications to assist the newcomer (you!) Begin without yanking your hair to hair loss because the program's manual is a bit too lean:

1. The very first thing you'll see is that the digital mat that appears just like your bodily pad. That is your digital design area and where the majority of the action will occur. Begin by clicking on some other form in the keypad overlay (the major box only in addition to the mat) and play with the picture. You will see huge circles around the contour. These are known as "selection manages" and allow you to control and distort the picture in each direction.

2. The next thing you'll see is the keypad overlay. This is the digital keyboard that changes depending on the cartridges you have chosen. Every time you click on one of them, the letters or shapes that appear on it will be displayed on your digital mat so you can play and trace exactly what you would like.

3. Third would be the two boxes just opposite to the keyboard overlay: the library of opportunities around the left and also the form properties box to its right. The opportunity library is precisely what its name implies, it is a sort of indicator of all the cartridges out there. You can design in any of those cartridges and also use letters or shapes from several cartridges in the same design, but you will have the ability to cut only with all the cartridges you have (not fashionable!... I get it). The outline properties box allows you to control the selected letters or shapes more precisely. You are able to provide them with X and Y coordinates (like in college), you can give them exact height and width, it is possible to rotate them can push them can weld them kern.

Chapter 10 Tools and Accessories of Cricut Machine

When you have a Cricut machine, there are a few tools that you would need which would make your crafting project easier and manageable. All these different tools help with cutting materials. The tools that you would require are:

Cricut Cutting Mat

For every Cricut Machine you have, the must-have item every crafter needs is a cutting mat. This cutting mat enables you to hold any material you use while the machine goes through cutting it. These mats come in different grip strengths and also varying sizes. You can differentiate it by the colors it comes in based on the grip, so you do not confuse them. Some projects would require you to use the StrongGrip mat, whereas some projects work better using a mat suitable based on the materials you are using, such as fabric.

The outcome of your project depends on the kind of mat you use, so choosing the right mat is imperative. The different types of mats available are the LightGrip Mat, StandardGrip Mat, StrongGrip Mat, and FabricGrip Mat.

Cricut Bright Pad

This Bright Pad includes a five-brightness setting adjustable LED light. It makes your crafting easier, and it aids in illuminating extremely fine lines for tracing. It is extremely useful when you are weeding, so if you find that weeding is a challenge, then the Cricut Bright Pad will solve this issue for you as it makes this process easier.

Cricut Pens

Cricut Pens come in different colors and a variety of sets that make DIY projects such as gift tags, cards, invitations, and banners so much more creative and beautiful. Crafters usually use these pens when they need to Write and Cut. You can get Metallic pens, Candy Shop pens, the Classic set, Gold set, and even one called the Seaside set.

Lint Roller

Yes, you read that right. Get yourself a lint roller. It is useful for removing any unwanted pet hairs, dust, or excess materials from your mats. Animal hairs are big problems as they stick to the adhesive mats like there is no tomorrow, but a lint roller works great if you want to get rid of them.

Scoring Stylus

Add a scoring stylus to your cart as soon as possible if you are a paper crafter. The tool is excellent for making paper baskets and boxes. It gives the products the professional, store-bought finish and makes them as easy to fold as the stylus already creates the grooves for folding your paper projects.

EasyPress

Invest in an EasyPress. This is perfect if you are interested in printing T-shirts or customizing pillowcases. Basically, anything you want to have printed, you are going to need one of these bad boys to do it. There are lots of bundles available on the Cricut website, and they can range from $119.99 (only the EasyPress) to $389.99 for a large bundle with everything you need to get started on your printing journey and so much more. The prices change depending on the size of the EasyPress, as well as the size of the bundle you wish to take.

Complete Starter Kit

The Complete Starter Kit is great if you don't feel like purchasing tools individually or if you'd rather follow protocol and purchase exactly what you need. The kit comes with all the essential items; that's why it is a great purchase. However, if you're tight on cash, buying the bare necessities will be best. This includes the materials you may require to start crafting, so you don't have to worry about any list of items that need to be bought.

Cartridge

Cartridges are designed to help with the keyboard overlay that is needed for designs. The DesignStudio that is downloadable on the computer will help with developing the design that you are looking for. Each cartridge is designed to have a booklet to help you with how to use it. Each cartridge will only work for that specific overlay; however, a company called Provo Craft designed a universal overlay cartridge that will help with this single-use overlay issue. This allows the DIY crafter to only have to learn one keyboard overlay instead of multiple, giving them a much better chance of being able to understand the Cricut machine easily. Each Cricut, whether a cake version or a paper version, has a specific set of parameters that will be set to use for cutting. This makes each one of the Cricut machines specific to their use and a unique tool to have.

Buy a cartridge or several. Please do invest in these. They are amazing, and they aren't that expensive if you look around for clearance sales or marked-down prices on Amazon. There are so many cartridges to choose from; it's like a never-ending pit of creativity. The selection ranges from themed cartridges to ones that only have fonts. It's great for any project, and it saves you the trouble of struggling with Design Space and creating your own designs. They also come in neat little boxes that are so easy to store and always look uniform.

Sharpies

Sharpies - you will not be sorry that you have them. Yes, the Cricut pens are cool, but they are overpriced. Purchasing some extra Sharpies – or any form of pens that can be manipulated into fitting into the pen holder – will work perfectly. You will have a variety of colors and save a couple of bucks in the process.

Doors

The door on your Cricut Cutter machine protects the machine when not in use. On many Cricut Cutter machines in various models, there is a compartment on the inside of the door to place any needed tools for crafting. If the doors on your Cricut cutter machine are not staying shut, make sure that you have taken out or unloaded any accessories in the machine's accessory clamp, which can cause the doors to remain open. If this is not the case or the doors of the machine will not open or stay open, take a picture or video and send it to the Help Center at Cricut.com.

Spatula

A spatula is used to lift the cut papers from the cutting mat. You can also use other related things like some stuffed cards. But, as a spatula is not expensive and specially designed tool, so it is recommended to use. It does not harm your cutting mat. Removing gross and sticky material from spatula is easy.

Adhesives

Choose the adhesive of your choice from any well-known brand. Sticky materials, such as adhesives, should not be ordinary, the purpose of gluing two things together must be fulfilled through your selected adhesive. Different sizes of glue coffee cups are available. Select any jumbo pack or coffee cup or according to your requirement. The drying time of glue also matters, so go for some very good adhesive.

Tapes

Without the adhesive tape, completing the task is almost impossible. Points to consider when selecting masking tape are: it must be free of chemicals or acids and it must be very sticky. Glue is an alternative to tape, but sometimes glue does not work as well as tape.

Scissors

Carry a pair of sharp scissors with you. Sharp enough to cut cards, ribbons and papers. You should purchase a sheath for the scissors. Place it out of reach of children and in a place where it will not be affected by moisture. Clean cutting of paper or cards really involves your decorative work.

Tweezers

Sometimes you have to deal with very small papers. Tweezers work effectively in holding that small piece of paper that usually becomes curled, curved, and torn during use. Sometimes additional use of glue sticks two papers that are hard to get separate tweezers are perfect helper at that time. Keep it while crafting, as you will need it.

Trimmers

Blades and guillotines are essential, as they help to cut papers very cleanly and to the desired shape without having to make extra effort to create a clean effect.

Paper and cardstock are comparatively thicker than paper. They are different things. Buying a stock gets you off the hook, whether you make test cuttings or throw it into making unusual shapes for the trace. They should be enough to complete all your tasks.

Blades

The blades are designed to cut specific textiles when using the Cricut. Every single Cricut machine that you can buy comes with your own specific blade for that machine. You can purchase other blades that would be even more useful for specific textiles. Many of them come with a German fine point carbide blade. This is a useful blade for all projects. However, you may want to invest in a deep-cut blade eventually. This one provides an effortless cutting of a much thicker textile such as leather and wood. There is an individual housing that will be used for this specific blade that is different from the one that comes with your machine, so keep that in mind. There is also an option or a fabric blade that is bonded. This is used to cut fabrics that are already stabilized with some sort of heat-pressed bonding. In the Cricut Maker, you will get a knife blade and a rotary as well. These do not work in other Cricut machines.

Keypad

The Cricut cartridge contains fonts and images often of a specific subject. The keyboard allows you to enter phrases and words to tell the Cricut what to cut out using the cartridge font.

Buttons

For the most part, all buttons are self-explanatory. The on button turns the machine on, the Cut button tells the machine to cut once the design is already in place, and the Stop button tells the Cricut machine to stop cutting once the design has been fully cut. It is important not to attempt to cut or press the cut button without a cutting mat in place and without a design and cartridge ready to use. Select the STOP button if you have made a mistake during the cutting process, the blade will stop cutting and you can then correct your mistake. The OFF button turns the machine off.

Roller Bar

The roller bar part of the Cricut Cutter machine has wheels called star wheels. The star wheels keep the materials from slipping when cutting. However, when cutting thick materials such as felt and foam, the star wheels can leave marks and nicks in the material. To avoid these star wheel marks move the star wheels to the right side of the rubber bar one at a time. If the cartridge gets in the way of this maneuver, turn off your Cricut cutter by selecting the OFF button and gently move the cartridge to either side. To make sure the material still does not go over the star wheels, make sure the material is at least one inch away from the right side of the rubber bar where the star wheels are now located.

Chapter 11 FAQ

1. Why Does Design Space Say That My Cricut machine is Already in Use When It's Not?

To resolve this, make sure that you've completed the New Machine Setup for your Cricut. Try Design Space in another browser. The two that work best are Google Chrome and Mozilla Firefox; if it doesn't work in one of those, try the other. If that doesn't clear the error, try a different USB port and USB cable. Disconnect the machine from the computer and turn it off. While it's off, restart your computer. After your computer restarts, reconnect the machine and turn it on. Wait a few moments, then try Design Space again. If you're still having the same problem, contact Cricut Member Care.

2. Why Doesn't My Cut Match the Preview in Design Space?

Test another image and see if the same thing happens. If it's only happening with one project, create a new project and start over or try a different image. If it happens with a second project, and your machine is connected with Bluetooth, disconnect that and plug it in with a USB cable. Larger projects may sometimes have difficulty communicating the cuts over Bluetooth. If you can't connect with USB or the problem is still occurring, check that your computer matches or exceeds the system requirements for running Design Space. If it doesn't, try the project on a different computer or mobile device that does. If your computer does meet the requirements, open Design Space in a different browser and try again. If the problem continues, try a different USB cable. Finally, if the issue still hasn't been resolved, contact Cricut Member Care.

3. What Do I Do If I Need to Install USB Drivers for My Cricut Machine?

Typically, the Cricut drivers are automatically installed when you connect them with a USB cable. If Design Space doesn't see your machine, you can try this to troubleshoot the driver installation. First, open Device Manager on your computer. You'll need to have administrator rights. For Windows 7, click Start, right-click on Computer, and select Manage. For Windows 8 and up, right-click on the Start icon and click Computer Management. Within Computer Management, click Device Manager on the left-hand side. Find your Cricut machine on the list—it should be listed under Ports, but it might be under Other Devices or Universal Serial Bus Controllers. Right-click on it and select Update Driver Software. In the box that pops up, select Browse My Computer.

In the box on the next screen, type in %APPDATA% and click Browse. Another box will pop up where you can search through folders. Find AppData and expand it. Click Roaming, then CricutDesignSpace, then Web, then Drivers, then CricutDrivers, and click OK. Click Next to install these drivers. Once it's finished, restart your computer. Once it's on, open Design Space again to see if it recognizes your machine.

4. Why Does My Cricut Maker Say the Blade is Not Detected?

Make sure that the tool in Clamp B is the same one Design Space recommends in the Load Tools step of the Project Preview screen. If you don't have that recommended tool, unload your mat and select Edit Tools on the Project Preview screen. Here, you can select a different tool. If the tool and the selection already match, carefully remove the tool from Clamp B and clean the reflective band on the housing. Reinstall it in the clamp and press the Go button. If that doesn't resolve the problem, remove the tool again, and clean the sensor inside the machine.

Reinstall the tool and press Go again. If the Maker still doesn't detect the blade, try a simple test project using a basic shape with one of the other tools. If that works, there may be something wrong with the drive housing of the original tool. If the problem continues with other tools, or you don't have another tool to test, trying uninstalling and reinstalling Design Space and retry your project. If the issue persists, or if you've discovered it's an issue with the tool housing, contact Cricut Member Care.

5. Why is My Cricut Machine Making a Grinding Noise?

If it's the carriage car making a loud noise after you press the cut button, and it sounds like the carriage might be hitting the side of the machine, record a short video of it and send it to Cricut Member Care. If the noise is coming from a brand-new machine the first time you use it, contact Cricut Member Care. Otherwise, make sure that you're using the original power cord that came with your machine. If the machine isn't getting the correct voltage, it may produce a grinding sound. If you are using the machine's power cord, adjust your pressure settings. If it's too high, it might produce an unusual sound. Decrease it in increments of 2–4, and do some test cuts. If it's still making the issue even after decreasing the cutting pressure, contact Cricut Member Care.

6. What If My Cricut is Making a Different Loud Noise?

Make sure that you don't have Fast Mode engaged for cutting or writing. If it's not on, take a short video of the problem to send to Cricut Member Care.

7. Why is My Mat Going into the Machine Crooked?

Check the roller bar to see if it's loose, damaged, or uneven. If it is, take a photo or video of it to send to Cricut Member Care. If the roller bar seems fine, make sure that you're using the right mat size for the machine. Next, make sure the mat is correctly lined up with the guides and that the edge is underneath the roller bar when you prepare to load it. If it's still loading crookedly even when properly lined up with the guides, try applying gentle pressure to the mat to get it under the roller bar once it starts. If none of this works, contact Cricut Member Care.

8. Why Isn't the Smart Set Dial Changing the Material in Design Space?

Make sure that the USB cable between the computer and the Cricut Explore is properly connected. If so, disconnect the Explorer from the computer and turn it off. Restart your computer. Once it's on, turn on the Explore, plug it into the computer, and try the cut again. If it still isn't changing the material, connect the USB cable to a different port on the computer. If it's still not working, try Design Space in multiple web browsers and see if the problem replicates. If it does, try an entirely different USB cable. Check for Firmware Updates for the Explore. If you don't have another USB cable, the Firmware Update doesn't help, or there are no Firmware Updates, contact Cricut Member Care.

9. What Do I Do If My Cricut Maker Stopped Partway Through a Cut?

If the Knife Blade stops cutting and the Go button is flashing, the Maker has encountered some sort of error. In Design Space, you'll get a notification that the blade is stuck. This might have been caused by the blade running into something like a knot or seam if too much dust or debris built up in the cut area or if the blade got into a gouge in the mat from a previous cut. To resume your project, do not unload the mat. This will lose your place in the project, and it will be impossible to get it lined up again. Check the cut area for dust or debris, and gently clean it. If there's dust on top of Clamp B, brush it off with a clean, dry paintbrush. Do not remove the blade. Once the debris is gone, press the Go button. The machine will take a moment to sense the Knife Blade again, and then it will resume cutting.

10. Why is My Fabric Getting Caught Under the Rollers?

Be sure to cut down any fabric so that it fits on your mat without going past the adhesive. If you have stuck the fabric and realize it's hanging past the adhesive, use a ruler and a sharp blade to trim it. Or, if it's the correct size but slightly askew, unstick it and reposition it.

11. Why Would My Cricut Maker Continuously Turn Off During Cuts?

This can happen from a build-up of static electricity while cutting foil and metal sheets. Makers in dry areas are more susceptible to this. Spritzing water in the air will dissipate the build-up. Be careful not to spray any water directly on the Maker. Using a humidifier or vaporizer in the area where you use your Maker can help avoid static build-ups. If this doesn't seem to be what's causing the issue, contact Cricut Member Care.

12. What Do I Do About a Failing or Incomplete Firmware Update?

Be sure to use a computer to install the firmware update and that you're connected with a USB cable rather than Bluetooth. Verify that the computer meets the minimum system requirements; if it doesn't, you'll need to use another computer that does. If it does and you're still having problems, disconnect the Cricut from your computer and turn it off. Restart the computer. Once it's back on, open Design Space and try the firmware update again. If it still freezes up or doesn't complete, try the update using a different web browser. The next step is to try another USB cable. If that doesn't help, or you don't have another USB cable to try, contact Cricut Member Care.

13. What Do I Do If My Cricut Machine Has Power Issues?

If your Cricut Maker, Cricut Explore One, or Cricut Explore Air 2 is having issues with power, these are the troubleshooting steps. If the machine doesn't have any power or only has it sometimes, make sure that the plug is completely plugged into the power port on the machine, the power adapter, and the wall outlet. The cutting mat can sometimes knock the power cable loose as it goes through the machine. You can avoid this by making sure the excess cord isn't bundled up behind the machine.

If everything is securely plugged in, make sure that you're using the genuine Cricut power cable that came with your machine and that the green light on the adapter is lit up. If you're not using the Cricut power cable, you can buy one or contact Cricut Member Care. If you are, try using a different wall outlet. If it's still having problems, try another Cricut power cable. If the issues continue even after this, take a short video of the issue happening and forward it to Cricut Member Care.

14. What Do I Do If I Have Issues with the Machine's Door?

If the door will not open or will not stay open, record a short video to forward to Cricut Customer Service. If the door will not close or will not stay closed, make sure there is no accessory loaded in the accessory clamp. If there is not, take a photo or short video to send to Cricut's Customer Service team.

Conclusion

Explorer Air 2 machine is very fast and will surprise you on your very first project. The machine has an upgraded material blade that works with over 10 types of materials. The cutting functionality of this circuit is wow while working with different materials. It can easily cut different types of material and finish the work on the desired materials. You can cut your project faster by making use of its fast mode and you can also step up things with its customizable options to customize its settings. There is also a software available that may work with the machine using their personal computers. This software is easy to use with a large number of designs and projects installed from which you can select the design or project you want to start the machine with.

From what I have seen this machine do, I will say that the Cricut Explorer Air 2 machine is one of the best if not the best smart cutting machine available.

The Cricut Explore Air 2 machine is a wireless design and cut system kind of device. It can cut different varieties of materials easily because it has a Smart set dial. Cricut Explore Air 2 machine is a fast mode machine that enables it to cut and write twice as fast according to the settings of the tools and the images you are cutting. To make effective use of the Fast Mode, you are advised to select the Fast Mode in the design space and set the material between Vinyl and Cardstock.

Accessories such as the blade, blade housing as well as accessory adapter are all pre-installed in the Cricut Explore Air 2 machine. You will find settings of the most common materials displayed on the dial, and there is an entire library of materials present in the Design space. You are advised to set the dial to custom.

The Cricut Explore Air 2 machine has adequate storage, which makes everything you need readily available in it. The Cricut Explore Air 2 machine is an automated machine that enables it to adjust the Smart Set dials for the user.

It also has a cup that helps in holding your tools and also has two accessory compartments, which are the small and large compartments. The smaller compartment has magnetic strips that help in holding additional housings and the accessory adapter.

The larger compartment helps in the storage of different Cricut tools. The Cricut Explore Air 2 machine is made up of cartridge ports. The cartridge helps in linking your cartridges to your Cricut account online, which, in turn, helps you access your images from any device.

Made in the USA
Columbia, SC
28 March 2023